Jason,
Thank you for the connection and partnership.
Do what you love, love what you do.
With gratitude,
Shannon

V.I.B.E.

WHERE VIBRANCY, INNOVATION, BRILLIANCE, AND EXCITEMENT ORIGINATE

SHANNON CASSIDY

Executive Coach · Speaker · Facilitator

DEDICATION:

To those who believe the journey
toward self discovery is worth the trip.
Find your V.I.B.E.

Potential Publishing
Philadelphia, PA
www.potenitalpublishing.com

Designed by Judith Nolan - Fitzpatrick Designs

ISBN: 978-0-9886122-3-5

Printed in the USA

What is it about a person that makes you drawn to them or repelled? How would you describe the energy someone provides or takes away? In a word: vibe. Vibe is the way an individual comes across. It's how you feel about an individual you don't even know. It's a presence. It's the experience of a person. Their impact. Aura. Affect.

Each of us have a vibe.
What does V.I.B.E. mean?

Your V.I.B.E. consists of four specific pieces.

YOUR VALUES.
YOUR INTERESTS.
YOUR BELIEFS.
YOUR ENERGY SOURCES.

PICTURE AN...
ICEBERG.

The scope, mass, true form, wonder and beauty of it lie beneath the surface.

Our V.I.B.E. is part of the mass beneath the surface.

The question isn't:
"Do you have a V.I.B.E. ?";
rather, it's,
"What is your V.I.B.E.?"

The answer to that question is found through self discovery and awareness.

This book is designed to take you on a journey. A discovery of what lies beneath and how that impacts you and others.

DARE TO EXPLORE!

[val·ue]

noun

plural noun: values

a person's principles or standards of behavior; one's judgment of what is important in life

Our values are the core principles that give meaning to our lives. When our values are aligned with our work activities, decisions and behavior, we are more satisfied. When our values are not aligned, we tend to experience a lack of contentment, certainty and control.

What are your core values? They are building blocks of your foundation. Not your wants, shoulds, fantasies or wishes. Values are essential to your life design and are non-negotiable.

"YOU ARE PURE POTENTIAL."
– Martin De Maat

OPEN YOUR ARMS TO CHANGE, BUT DON'T LET GO OF YOUR *values.*

- DALAI LAMA

HUMOR	PARTICIPATION	COLLABORATION
PERFORMANCE	PARTNERSHIP	CELEBRATION
PRODUCTIVITY	COMMUNITY	SERVICE
PERSONAL POWER / MASTERY	CONTRIBUTION	FREEDOM
EXCELLENCE	CONNECTION	FREE SPIRIT
ACKNOWLEDGMENT	FOCUS	LOVE
ROMANCE	LIGHTNESS	RECOGNITION
SPIRITUALITY	HARMONY	EMPOWERMENT
ACCOMPLISHMENT	FULL SELF-EXPRESSION	ORDERLINESS
INTEGRITY	FORWARD THE ACTION	CREATIVITY
HONESTY	INDEPENDENCE	SUCCESS
NURTURING	ACCURACY	JOY
BEAUTY	AUTHENTICITY	DIRECTNESS
DIVERSITY	RISK TAKING	TRUST
TRADITION	PEACE	TO BE KNOWN
ELEGANCE	GROWTH	VITALITY
AESTHETICS	INTEGRITY	RESILIENCY
CELEBRATION	LOYALTY	ABUNDANCE
GENEROSITY	LEADERSHIP	TRANQUILITY
COLLABORATION	MODERATION	MULTICULTURALISM
PASSION	INDIVIDUALISM	BALANCE
OWNERSHIP / SELF-RESPONSIBILITY	ACHIEVEMENT	CERTAINTY
HEALTH / WELL BEING	POWER	TEAMWORK
PURSUIT OF KNOWLEDGE	LEARNING	INFLUENCE
INDEPENDENCE	BELONGING	INTEGRITY
COMMITMENT	CONTRIBUTING	RESPECT
ENVIRONMENTAL AWARENESS	RESPONSIBILITY	EQUALITY
SELF RESPECT	GIVING TO COMMUNITY	JUSTICE
STATUS	HONESTY	ADVENTUROUS
INITIATING	ADVOCACY	TIME
ANALYTICAL	ORGANIZING	CHALLENGE
PHYSICAL	CONCEPTUALIZING	PROBLEM-SOLVING
CREATIVE	PUBLIC CONTACT	DECISION-MAKING
RESEARCH	DETAILED	RISK-TAKING
HELPING	VARIETY	AUTONOMY
PERSONAL SAFETY	BENEFITS	PREDICTABLE
COMFORTABLE INCOME	QUIET	EXCITEMENT
RELAXED	FUN	COMMUNITY

OUR PROBLEM IS NOT
to find
BETTER VALUES
but to
BE FAITHFUL
to the ones
WE PROFESS.

– JOHN W. GARDNER

THE VALUE OF KNOWING YOUR VALUES:

IF YOU DON'T KNOW WHO YOU ARE, YOU CAN'T BE TRUE TO YOURSELF.

Sounds obvious, but many of us go through life without taking the time to identify what truly matters.

IT MAKES DECISION-MAKING EASIER.

When contemplating choices, filter them through your values. How does each choice align with your values? If both choices are congruent with your values, which one aligns most with your top priorities?

IT HELPS YOU IDENTIFY PEOPLE, SITUATIONS, TASKS AND THINGS TO ATTRACT OR AVOID.

Clarifying your core values helps define desires and dreads. Desires are what you want most: life partner, career path, close acquaintances, and personal brand. Dreads are the things you want to avoid: unethical situations, white lies, big lies, toxic relationships and actions harmful to others. Use your core values to guide your decisions to stay consistent with who you are and what you believe.

IT GIVES YOU A SENSE OF PEACE.

Clarifying your values and living your life in alignment with those values provides an inner peace and tranquility that allows you to move confidently through life.

WHEN YOUR VALUES ARE CLEAR TO YOU, MAKING DECISIONS BECOMES EASIER.

- ROY DISNEY

IT ALLOWS YOU TO KNOW YOURSELF.

We know when we're not being true to ourselves. We experience a vague sense of uneasiness and become defensive. When we are clear about our values, we respond with greater certainty, stability and authenticity.

IT ALLOWS YOU TO GET RID OF GOALS THAT AREN'T REALLY YOURS.

Take an objective look at your goals. Are they truly reflective of your heart and desires? Perhaps your current list of goals includes things you think you 'should' want. Let them go. The guilt associated with these goals is wasting energy you could be investing to achieve what you really want.

IT ALLOWS YOU TO BE VERY CLEAR ABOUT THE STANDARDS YOU SET FOR YOURSELF.

What are your standards? If there were an instruction manual for you, what would it say are the "Do's" and "Don'ts"? What behavioral standards, social courtesies, and manners do you expect from others? What is intolerable to you? How do you respond when someone or something is in conflict with your values?

IT ALLOWS YOU TO BE VERY CLEAR ABOUT BOUNDARIES

Boundaries are what other people cannot do to or around you. The behavior that is least acceptable to you is likely violating your values. Clarity about your values allows establishing and enforcing boundaries to be painless. You're not trying to change people. You are simply enforcing behavior that's acceptable around you.

I think the world would be a lot better off if more people were to define themselves in terms of their own standards and values and not what other people said or thought about them.

- HILLARY CLINTON

THE MOST EFFECTIVE WAY TO DISCOVER YOUR CORE VALUES IS TO ASK THESE QUESTIONS:

WHAT CAN YOU
NOT TOLERATE?

• • •

WHAT MAKES
YOU CRAZY?

[MINING FOR VALUES]

WRITE THE LIST OF THINGS YOU CANNOT TOLERATE. NOW, DRILL DOWN TO DISCOVER THE CORE VALUE DEEP BENEATH THE SURFACE.

EXAMPLES

I cannot tolerate lying.

It drives me crazy when people are late.

I cannot tolerate rude behavior.

It drives me crazy when people are lazy.

CORE VALUES

honesty · truth telling

promptness · respect · time management

respect · compassion · dignity

work ethic · dedication · commitment

WHAT CAN'T YOU TOLERATE?

1._____

2._____

3._____

CORE VALUE:

_____

_____

_____

WHAT DRIVES YOU CRAZY?

1._____

2._____

3._____

CORE VALUE:

_____

_____

_____

[MINING FOR VALUES]

>>> **EXAMPLE** <<<

HONESTY

INTEGRITY

RESPONSIBILITY

LOYALTY

TRUST

LOVE

PLAYFULNESS

COMPASSION

QUALITY SERVICE

MY TOP 5 CORE VALUES ARE:

1. _____

2. _____

3. _____

4. _____

5. _____

HAPPINESS

is that state of
consciousness
which proceeds
from the
achievement of
one's **VALUES."**

- Ayn Rand

Don't let your special character and values, the secret that you know and no one else does,

THE TRUTH

- don't let that get swallowed up by the great chewing of complacency.

– Aesop

[in·ter·est]

noun

plural noun: interests

a. state of curiosity or concern about or attention to something

b. Something, such as a quality, subject, or activity, that evokes this mental state

What do you really enjoy?   Think about activities, discussion topics, areas of study, products, services and hobbies you find most interesting.

Do you love singing in the shower?

Hosting dinner parties?

Helping friends solve problems?

Cooking?

Gardening?

Playing music?

Taking things apart?

Putting things together?

Reading?

Reflecting?

Conversing?

Writing?

INTERESTS

"ENTHUSIASM IS CONTAGIOUS. START AN EPIDEMIC.**"**

– bumper sticker

WHAT WOULD YOU ATTEMPT TO DO «««««««««««««« IF YOU KNEW YOU COULD NOT FAIL?

– UNKNOWN

MY TOP 5 INTERESTS ARE:

What do you really love? Sometimes finding the answer to that question is harder than we think. Try finishing these sentences to help get you started.

I can hardly wait to....
I really lose track of time when...
I always find the time/money for...
The best gift someone could give me would be...

1._____

2._____

3._____

4._____

5._____

IF YOU COULD ADD ONE MORE HOUR TO EACH DAY, WHAT WOULD YOU DO WITH IT?

60 MINUTES. 60 MINUTES. 60 MINUTES. 60 MINUTES. 60 MINUTES. 60 MINUTES. 60 MINUTES. 60 MINUTES.

IF YOU CAN
dream it,
YOU CAN
DO IT.

— WALT DISNEY

[INTEREST #1]
REFLECTION

INTEREST #1 _____

WHAT ABOUT THIS ACTIVITY IS SO INTERESTING TO YOU?

_____

_____

_____

_____

WHAT EMOTIONS DO YOU EXPERIENCE WHEN YOU DO THIS ACTIVITY?

_____

_____

_____

_____

WHAT COULD MAKE THE ACTIVITY EVEN BETTER?

_____

_____

_____

_____

INSPIRATION
and
GENIUS
– one and the same
– VICTOR HUGO

[INTEREST #2]
REFLECTION

INTEREST #2 _____

WHAT ABOUT THIS ACTIVITY IS SO INTERESTING TO YOU?

_____
_____
_____
_____

WHAT EMOTIONS DO YOU EXPERIENCE WHEN YOU DO THIS ACTIVITY?

_____
_____
_____
_____

WHAT COULD MAKE THE ACTIVITY EVEN BETTER?

_____
_____
_____
_____

NOBODY EVER DIED OF LAUGHTER.

– MAX BEERBOHM

INTEREST #3 _____

WHAT ABOUT THIS ACTIVITY IS SO INTERESTING TO YOU?

_____

_____

_____

_____

WHAT EMOTIONS DO YOU EXPERIENCE WHEN YOU DO THIS ACTIVITY?

_____

_____

_____

_____

WHAT COULD MAKE THE ACTIVITY EVEN BETTER?

_____

_____

_____

_____

LEAP
AND
THE NET
WILL APPEAR
- ZEN SAYING

[INTEREST #4]
REFLECTION

INTEREST #4

WHAT ABOUT THIS ACTIVITY IS SO INTERESTING TO YOU?

WHAT EMOTIONS DO YOU EXPERIENCE WHEN YOU DO THIS ACTIVITY?

WHAT COULD MAKE THE ACTIVITY EVEN BETTER?

[be·lief]

noun
plural noun: beliefs

a. an acceptance that a statement
   is true or that something exists

b. trust, faith, or confidence in
   someone or something

We have beliefs about everything. You have beliefs about others, politics, economy, religion, justice, technology, etc. To best discover your V.I.B.E. consider the beliefs you have about yourself. These inner beliefs range from job security, life partner, career choices, circumstances, fear, limitations, self-identity and extent of capabilities.

To narrow down the scope, let's focus only on the beliefs you have about your self-identity.

BELIEFS

"WE ARE BORN
BELIEVING.
A MAN BEARS BELIEFS AS
A TREE BEARS APPLES."
– Ralph Waldo Emerson

YOU SEE
EVERYTHING
IS ABOUT
BELIEF.
WHATEVER WE
BELIEVE
RULES OUR EXISTENCE,
RULES OUR LIFE.

— DON MIGUEL RUIZ

I AM
STATEMENT

Please complete at least *(minimum)* 25 sentences that begin with I am... Personal/ Professional – all together. Include anything that comes to mind, as long as it adheres to the rules.

RULES OF ENGAGEMENT:

- Must be positive.
- Must be present tense.
- Must be future/ visionary/ ideal state of you.
- Include strengths you are already aware of.
- Use rich/ robust/ exciting adjectives. ("Good" won't work.)
- How do you really want to be?

WHILE PRODUCING YOUR "I AM" STATEMENT - TAKE THIS IN AND HOLD IT CLOSE:

"Our deepest fear is not that we are inadequate. Our deepest fear is that we are powerful beyond measure. It is our light, not our darkness that most frightens us. We ask ourselves, Who am I to be brilliant, gorgeous, talented, fabulous? Actually, who are you not to be? You are a child of God. Your playing small does not serve the world. There is nothing enlightened about shrinking so that other people won't feel insecure around you. We are all meant to shine, as children do. We were born to make manifest the glory of God that is within us. It's not just in some of us; it's in everyone. And as we let our own light shine, we unconsciously give other people permission to do the same. As we are liberated from our own fear, our presence automatically liberates others."

FROM "A RETURN TO LOVE", BY MARIANNE WILLIAMSON.

PLEASE COMPLETE AT LEAST 25 SENTENCES THAT BEGIN WITH I AM...
PERSONAL/PROFESSIONAL – ALL TOGETHER. INCLUDE ANYTHING THAT
COMES TO MIND, AS LONG AS IT ADHERES TO THE RULES OF ENGAGEMENT.

[I AM]

I AM _____

I AM _____

I AM _____

I AM _____

I AM _____

I AM _____

I AM _____

I AM _____

I AM _____

I AM _____

I AM _____

I AM _____

I AM _____

I AM _____

I AM _____

I AM _____

"WITHIN YOU RIGHT NOW IS
THE POWER TO DO THINGS YOU
NEVER DREAMED POSSIBLE.
THIS POWER BECOMES
AVAILABLE TO YOU JUST AS
SOON AS YOU CAN CHANGE
YOUR BELIEFS."

- Dr. Maxwell Maltz

I AM _____

I AM _____

I AM _____

I AM _____

I AM _____

I AM _____

I AM _____

I AM _____

I AM _____

I AM _____

I AM _____

I AM _____

I AM _____

I AM _____

I AM _____

I AM _____

WHAT ARE YOUR
BELIEFS?

CHOOSE 5-10.

>>> **EXAMPLE** <<<

I AM ENERGETIC

I AM PASSIONATE

I AM FOCUSED

I AM PROFESSIONAL

I AM ADAPTABLE

I AM STRATEGIC

I AM THOUGHTFUL

I AM CURIOUS

I AM AMBITIOUS

I am _____

I am _____

I am _____

I am _____

I am _____

I am _____

I am _____

I am _____

I am _____

I am _____

"Often people attempt to live their lives backwards: they try to have more things, or more money, in order to do more of what they want so they will be happier. The way it actually works is the reverse. You must first 'be who you really are' then do what you love to do, in order to have what you want."
- MARGARET YOUNG

The formula for success is

BE,
DO,
HAVE.

IF WE SEEK ABUNDANCE, WE MUST BE ABUNDANT IN SPIRIT.

YOUNG.
OLD.
JUST WORDS.
- GEORGE BURNS

LIVE YOUR BELIEFS
AND YOU CAN
TURN THE WORLD
AROUND.
- HENRY DAVID THOREAU

40

IT'S NOT THE EVENTS OF OUR LIVES THAT SHAPE US, BUT OUR BELIEFS AS TO WHAT THOSE EVENTS MEAN. *- TONY ROBBINS*

ENERGY SOURCES. ENERGY SOURCES. ENERGY SOURCES. ENERGY SOURCES. ENERGY SOURCES. ENERGY SOURCES. ENERGY SOURCES. ENERGY SOURCES. ENERGY SOURCES. ENERGY SOURCES. ENERGY SOURCES. ENERGY SOURCES. ENERGY SOURCES. ENERGY SOURCES. ENERGY SOURCES.

[en·er·gy]

noun

a. ability to do things: the ability or power to work or make an effort; vigor

b. liveliness and forcefulness; forceful effort

c. a vigorous effort or action

With the fast-paced world we live in today and the advancement of technology, we take pride in our ability to multi-task. We often feel starved for time and our minds are consumed with all we need to get done in a day. It's no wonder we feel drained of energy and unfocused.

Energy is the primary resource for life and business. Everything we do – from interacting with colleagues and making important decisions to spending time with our families - requires energy. Without the right quantity, quality, focus and force of energy, we are compromised in any activity we undertake.

WE BEGIN TO REALIZE WE ARE ENERGY ITSELF WITH ALL OF ITS POSSIBILITIES."

- Ted Andrews

SOURCES OF
ENERGY

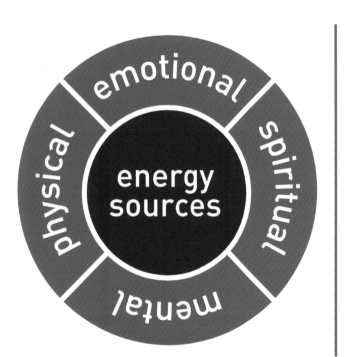

We have four separate but related sources of energy: **physical, emotional, mental and spiritual**. All four sources depend on each other. To perform at our best, we must skillfully manage each of these interconnected dimensions of energy. Subtract any one from the equation and our capacity to fully perform is diminished.

[FINDING YOUR] ENERGY SOURCE

WHAT IS YOUR FUEL?

_____
_____
_____
_____

WHAT MAKES YOU COME ALIVE?

_____
_____
_____
_____

WHAT FILLS UP YOUR ENERGY WELL?

_____
_____
_____
_____

WHAT IS YOUR BATTERY PACK?

_____
_____
_____
_____

WHAT'S YOUR MOTIVATION?

Each of us is fueled by something. We are all motivated by different things for different reasons. Money is the myth of motivation. We are led to believe that people only care about money. Provided an individual has enough money to live, the truth is that people are driven by a sense of purpose, belonging and contribution.

WHAT MOTIVATES YOU?

_____

_____

_____

_____

_____

WHERE DO YOU GET YOUR ENERGY?

_____

_____

_____

_____

_____

IF YOU COULD WAKE UP TOMORROW WITH SIGNIFICANTLY MORE
POSITIVE, FOCUSED ENERGY TO INVEST AT WORK AND WITH YOUR
FAMILY, HOW MUCH WOULD THAT CHANGE YOUR LIFE FOR THE BETTER?
WHAT WOULD YOU DO WITH THAT BOOST?

_____

_____

_____

_____

_____

_____

_____

AS A LEADER IN YOUR ORGANIZATION *(LEADERSHIP ISN'T A TITLE, IT'S
A SHARED RESPONSIBILITY)*, HOW VALUABLE WOULD IT BE TO BRING
MORE POSITIVE ENERGY AND PASSION TO THE WORKPLACE? HOW
WOULD MORE POSITIVE ENERGY AFFECT YOUR RELATIONSHIPS AND
THE QUALITY OF SERVICE YOU DELIVER?

_____

_____

_____

_____

_____

_____

bottom line...

More effective energy
management
will allow you to be more

PHYSICALLY ENERGIZED,

EMOTIONALLY CONNECTED,

MENTALLY FOCUSED &

SPIRITUALLY ALIGNED.

ENERGY SOURCES

CHOOSE 5.

>>> **EXAMPLE** <<<

EXERCISE

MEDITATION

SLEEP

NUTRITION

FRIENDS

READING

QUIET

DANCING

I AM ENERGIZED BY:

1._____

2._____

3._____

4._____

5._____

[WHAT NOT TO WANT...]

Sometimes it's easier for us to understand what we want by identifying what we don't want and inverting it. Here are examples, from *The Human Performance Institute*, of what it's like to lack energy in the four areas:

PHYSICAL, EMOTIONAL, MENTAL, AND SPIRITUAL.

PHYSICAL

- Not a priority
- Lack of routine
- Busy schedule
- Feel aches and pains
- Lack of commitment to fitness and nutrition
- Put off exercise
- Overweight
- Caffeine addicted

Our lives are the sum total of the choices we have made.
- Wayne Dyer

EMOTIONAL

- Negativity
- Criticism
- Taking things personally
- Lack of personal time... work during personal time
- Second guessing
- Lack of ownership
- Deny problems exist

People are just about as happy as they make up their minds to be.
- Abraham Lincoln

• • •

All the happiness you ever find lies in you.
- Anonymous

THE ENERGY OF THE MIND IS THE ESSENCE OF LIFE.
- Aristotle

"MOTIVATION
IS WHAT GETS YOU STARTED.
HABIT
IS WHAT KEEPS YOU GOING. "

-Jim Ryun

MENTAL

- Lack of sleep
- Poor time management
- Lack of time due to urgency
- Allowing distractions
- Lack of motivation and energy
- Justify/Explain purpose or role

*Knowing others is intelligence;
knowing yourself is true wisdom.
Mastering others is strength;
mastering yourself is true power.*
        - Tao Te Ching

• • •

*By your thoughts you are daily,
even hourly, building your life;
you are carving your destiny.*
        -Ruth Barrick Golden

SPIRITUAL

- Stuck in a bad spot without hope
- Lack of time to reflect and refresh
- Blurred vision
- A sense of not making a difference
- Not connecting with your role/purpose
- Lacking sense of unique strengths and gifts
- False sense of control

*Infuse your life with action. Don't
wait for it to happen. Make it
happen. Make your own future.
Make your own hope. Make your
own love. And whatever your
beliefs, honor your creator, not
by passively waiting for grace to
come down from upon high, but by
doing what you can to make grace
happen... yourself, right now, right
down here on Earth.*
        - Bradley Whitford

ULTIMATE HAPPINESS INCLUDES:

PHYSICAL ENERGY

Fitness

Nutrition

Rest & Recovery

Vitality

EMOTIONAL ENERGY

Interpersonal

Self-Esteem/Confidence

Responses to highs and lows

Managing Adversity/
Realistic Optimism

MENTAL ENERGY

Creativity/Curiosity

Focus/Concentration

Logical/
Solution Based Thinking

Mental Preparation

SPIRITUAL ENERGY

Commitment/Passion

Principle Centered/Ethical

Vision/Purpose

Sense of belonging
and self worth

HABITS

CONNECTION AND COMMITMENT
REQUIRE POSITIVE RITUALS
AND PRECISE BEHAVIORS THAT
BECOME AUTOMATIC OVER TIME.

THE ROLE OF RITUALS:

- Only 5% of our behaviors are consciously self-regulated.
- Behavior is largely a function of habit and routine
- Rituals are acquired with repetition

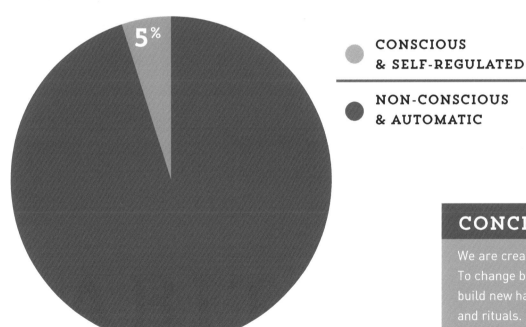

5%

CONSCIOUS
& SELF-REGULATED

NON-CONSCIOUS
& AUTOMATIC

CONCLUSION:

We are creatures of habit.
To change behavior, we must
build new habits, routines
and rituals.

The Human Performance Institute

THE CHAINS OF HABIT ARE TOO WEAK TO BE FELT
UNTIL THEY ARE TOO STRONG TO BE BROKEN.

- Samuel Johnson

[SELF COMMENTS]

WHAT ACTIVITIES DO YOU FIND HELP YOU RELAX AND
REGENERATE YOUR ENERGY?

_____

_____

_____

_____

WHAT DO YOU SEE AS THE BIGGEST PERSONAL OBSTACLE TO
HAVING MORE ENERGY AND BEING FULLY ENGAGED AT WORK?

_____

_____

_____

_____

WHAT'S ONE NEW HABIT YOU WILL BUILD TO IMPROVE YOUR
ENERGY MANAGEMENT?

_____

_____

_____

_____

THE WORLD IS A BETTER
PLACE BECAUSE I AM HERE;
THE ENERGY THAT I RADIATE
INTO THIS WORLD IS A
GIFT BEYOND MY OWN
UNDERSTANDING.

- JONATHAN LOCKWOOD HUIE

MEANING IS THE MOVIE YOU PRODUCE FROM YOUR CURRENT CIRCUMSTANCES. CREATE SOMETHING WORTH WATCHING!

- SHANNON CASSIDY

CREATING YOUR

V.I.B.E.

[PUTTING IT ALL TOGETHER]

[THE FORMULA]

MY V.I.B.E. INCLUDES:

VALUES:

from page 15

1. _____

2. _____

3. _____

4. _____

5. _____

INTERESTS:

from page 21

1. _____

2. _____

3. _____

4. _____

5. _____

BELIEFS:

choose your top 3 from page 38

I am _____

I am _____

I am _____

ENERGY SOURCE:

from page 49

1. _____

2. _____

3. _____

4. _____

5. _____

[REFLECTION]

VALUES

1 · · · · · · · · 2 · · · · · · · · 3 · · · · · · · · 4 · · · · · · · · 5

INTERESTS

1 · · · · · · · · 2 · · · · · · · · 3 · · · · · · · · 4 · · · · · · · · 5

BELIEFS

1 · · · · · · · · 2 · · · · · · · · 3 · · · · · · · · 4 · · · · · · · · 5

ENERGY

1 · · · · · · · · 2 · · · · · · · · 3 · · · · · · · · 4 · · · · · · · · 5

┤SCALE├

1: This component is **not at all reflected in my life.**

2: This component is **sometimes reflected in my life.**

3: This component is **occasionally reflected in my life.**

4: This component is **reflected in my life very often.**

5: This component is **absolutely reflected in my life every day.**

[REFLECTION]

WHAT WOULD NEED TO HAPPEN TO MAKE ALL FOUR SECTIONS OF
YOUR V.I.B.E. A FIVE? WHAT SMALL STEPS COULD YOU TAKE TO MAKE
PROGRESS IN EACH OF THE COMPONENTS THIS WEEK?

V.
I.
B.
E.

VALUES:
How could your daily life more fully reflect your core values? Which one needs the most attention? What can you do to honor it? If it's honesty, tell the truth with everyone. No white lies, no avoidance of detail – say what you mean and mean what you say.

INTERESTS :
Which of your interests have gotten lost? How much time can you allocate to one of your interests this week? Schedule time. Give yourself permission to spend time on things of interest.

BELIEFS:
You produced an "I am" statement on page 38. How can you deeply relate to it? Write your top three statements on a Post-it® note. Put it on your mirror, in your wallet, on your computer screen – wherever you'll see it! Read it out loud every day. Remind yourself about who you are.

ENERGY SOURCES:
Which one or two sources from your list help you to feel the most energized? If it's sleep, figure out what time you need to wake up, count back 7-8 hours and go to bed at that time. If it's music, create a new playlist to wake you up when you need a lift. Pick one energy source to focus on this week.

Knowing who you are is more important than knowing what you do. Make choices that align with who you are, what you value, your interests, beliefs about yourself and what makes you come alive! NEVER FORGET:

EVERY STEP COUNTS.

TO YOUR WELLBEING!

Journey to discover the unique
intricacies of your iceberg.

The depth of you is majestic...

FIND YOUR

V.I.B.E.

about the author
SHANNON CASSIDY

Executive Coach Shannon Cassidy has a proven track record of creating targeted and sustainable growth for national and international corporate leaders. Author of **The 5 Degree Principle** and co-author of **Discover Your Inner Strengths,** Shannon demonstrates how making small, incremental changes can help you achieve amazing results. With her many years of success, coupled with her belief in human potential, Shannon delivers powerful lessons with actionable takeaways.

Shannon is the founder and CEO of bridge between inc., a specialized executive development firm. Her expertise in behavioral excellence and leadership effectiveness has made her a much sought-after Executive Coach and Keynote Speaker.

V.I.B.E. - COACHING

Executive Coaching clients receive V.I.B.E. as one of the many resources distributed throughout their program. V.I.B.E. is a guide for the coaching process to help clients discover who they are and what makes them tick. Everyone has a battery pack and needs an energy charge.

V.I.B.E. - OUR PROGRAMS

Finding your V.I.B.E. is an essential component to many of our training programs and can be incorporated in these customized offerings:
- *The 5 Degree Principle: How Small Changes Lead to Big Results*
- *Staying Essential: Be the CEO of Your Career*
- *The Story of Success: How Perception Impacts Progress*
- *Communicating for Results: Style Preference and Adaptation*
- *Leading with Strengths: Maximize Your Potential*
- *The Power of Networking: Developing Who You Know*
- *Managing Corporate Politics: How to Play the Game*

V.I.B.E. - YOUR PROGRAMS

V.I.B.E. is the perfect resource to provide for team members. The content can be facilitated at:
- *Professional Development Meetings*
- *Business Off-Sites*
- *Executive Retreats*
- *Quarterly Meetings*
- *Annual Summits*
- *Team Building Programs*
- *Personal Development Planning Sessions*
- *Personal Improvement Planning Sessions*
- *One-on-One Coaching Meetings*

For more information on our programs please visit:
www.bridgebetween.com

 bridgebetweeninc  @shannoncassidy